If winter comes

Shelley Memorial Project
International Poetry Competition 2024

Published 2024 by Earthy Little Acorns Press
Station Road, Billingshurst, West Sussex, England.

Printed and bound by JR Print, Horsham

A CIP catalogue record for this book is available from the British Library

ISBN number: 978-1-0687570-1-3

Poems

Mood disorder

'Mood disorder' the psychiatrist wrote
But look at nature with her moods labile,
No one tells her how she should feel.
When half of my mind is tilted away from the sun,
An ego alien ice seizes control.
I have all the appearance of a frozen lake,
Lalique-like,
As though someone stole
The purest soul
And set it in glass.

Thoughts will not thaw,
Little can grow
And like leaves imprisoned in winter's strass
I cannot escape the white coats of snow.

Then all of a sudden from the safety of the hibernacle
I am roused by the radiance of those yellow flowers,
Chartreuse bullets that fire at will,
The ammunition of the daffodil.
Yet still I am vulnerable like the neck of a lamb,
My brain as fragile as the cherry blossom cloud
That weds me to a kind of happiness
Though I have barely left the shroud.

Soon the daffodil dies but the light remains,
No longer can I bask in her artificial rays.
Instead I look to the hands of honeysuckle,
How in their robes of Buddhist orange
They faithfully accept the illumination above
And I wonder if I too am worthy of such love.

But before I reach an answer my true colours arrive
And I learn that to fall is really to rise,
That surrounded by death I can still feel alive.

'Mood disorder' the psychiatrist wrote
But look at nature with her moods labile,
Though she cycles and changes
She is ever beautiful, ever worthwhile.

Sarah Mills

Winter Has A Wish For You

We watch in awe as nature reveals the view,
leaves fall in flurries, beguiling tears yearn,
a striptease, a beautiful striptease, slowly revealing
all the magnificence, an extraordinary display
of chutzpah, to show the deepest ravishing landscapes
at the trees expense, just hollow ghosts now,
stark against deepest glowing low winter sun,
the last pastel blues an endless prophecy of some
distant future, this beautiful melancholy, this majesty,
this terrible beauty, as bitter winds blow winter.

We feel alive as we see our breath as spectres,
surreal sunrise mysteries into the freezing air,
breathing out our ghosts, lung fragments of regrets,
noticing every crunch of ground, every jewel
glinting on the dewy grass, every spider's web
caught by bright sunshine, diamonds mesmerising
and enticing, fool's gold, but we are not fooled,
touch them and they disappear, despair, despair,
we are aware, of every single heightened moment,
by auburn miracles cascading, summoning us to sleep.

Peter Devonald

getting the summer clothes out of storage
You were still alive
     when I wore these last—
defiantly, on holiday although
     you couldn't come, your stiffened lungs long past
exertion, in-flight air, the drive
on narrow roads wound high above
the turquoise sea. Not even love
     could get you there and so,
     reluctantly, you watched me go.

I wash creased dresses,
     peg them out to dry.
Watching them flap in April air, I grieve
     your loneliness, your hurt-seized life: the *whys*,
the long, terrible distresses
you never could exhale, which left
you smaller than yourself, bereft.
     Spring asks me to believe
     that death can offer full reprieve.

.

Later, in the balm
     of evening, I take
the board and iron out, smoothing each crease
     from the worn, sun-bleached cloth. Nothing can make
them bright again—undo time's harm—
but they're soft now, and clean, and sing
the beauty song of tended things
     loved, lived-in; and released
     from winter's clasp; and part of peace.

Lucy Crispin

7

Here she comes!

Oh, here she comes!
With her light and her warmth.
Her soft, gentle breeze
Begins to tease.
A Siren of the sun -
The beckoning has begun.
Flowers start to bloom
Removing the gloom
Of the cold, dark enemy that came before her.

She brings a sense of hope and promise
As nature gifts new life.
Welcome rain helps to nourish
Blossom and bulbs begin to flourish.
She shares in the sweet birdsong -
Fledglings flustering, with a whistling chirrup
Industrious bees buzz and bustle
Paths carpeted with yellow daffodils
Their trumpets perfectly poised.

As she hands the baton to her reliable friend
Who promises long evenings that never end
Who rises majestically with a scorching glow
A phenomenal Phoenix, her haunting melody to bestow.
This seasoned chum
Brings a brighter, more fierce sun.
With folk toiling and mowing

And shrubs relentlessly growing
She brings people together
In a frisky abandon of garments and detritus
Feeding the greedy, gossiping gulls.

Unexpectedly, the evenings darken.
There's a sudden chill in the air.
The Thunderbird arrives to command our skies
Bringing gusts and gales with their howls and their cries.
She brings with her a lush new palette
Of red, orange, brown and yellow
As the world sets to work to prepare for its foe.
Squirrels hustle
Leaves fall and rustle
Laying a colourful blanket over our Earth.
Beaks and paws gather twigs, fruit and nuts
And our feathered friends swarm off to warmer climes
While others build shelter and bide their time.

Then all too quickly she emerges.
A monochrome, ethereal creature
Her icy heart turning everything white and dark.
This graceful Griffin swoops in
And claims the land with her frosty claws
Her unrelenting strength destroying all in her path.
The World takes cover.
And waits for the freezing onslaught to be over.

Caroline Berry

We Need To Talk About Summer

Sumer always reminds me of the end of childhood,
broken glass, shattered lives, endless rain on holiday,
waiting inside reeking cars, praying for quiet miracles,
glimpses of deserted saturated broken beaches,
umbrellas blown to the winds, arguments, quarrels,
fish and chips wrapped in newspapers, staining hands,
the perfect metaphor for summer, words stain, strain,
smeared onto flesh, greasy oily doubts, strange images,
sadness, sorrows, slamming doors, green windows, green
amusement arcades, Ferris wheels turns in a hurricane.

Afterwards, deep silence. I thought Mother would know,
that she'd notice the damage done, look at my face, please,
look at my face, inscriptions as clear as newspaper stains.
I was sure this would be the moment it all changed, now
would be the time of love and care, she'd notice me,
notice the damage done, but she was on the phone again
to someone else, someone she cared for, made her happy.
We walked on broken pavements covered in pot holes,
indentations, cracks and neglect, I skipped to avoid them,
but we all have to face unpalatable truths eventually.

Deep blue skies just lie to me, finally there is summer
just as I fall into deepest winter. Mother wants the beach
to luxuriate in nostalgia of childhood, that boat has sailed
for me now, lost at sea from the storm before, violent
and unattainable. We lie on the beach as I lie in my head,
Summer will always be a certain misery to me, watching
the horizon of the sea, wondering with enchantment where
I can run in the future, hide where all the clouds and fog go,
underneath the glowering skies, petulant reds and oranges,
a memory of a lawn mower, broken, in an enchanted sea.

Peter Devonald

Seasons

Summer arrived slow as a snake evolving
Through millennia, she dressed in colourful clothes:
The liquid light of autumnal onions,
Vivacious spring hint of daffodil,
Passionate flame of a winter blood orange.
Her parasol wore a rainbow
In case of inclement weather.

Autumn woke like a lurcher wrapped-up
In a brown paper bag; her bronze and crimson eyes
Resembled lightning during rain: gash of red on rash of grey,
But a sudden spring in her step created a late summer
Of fool's gold, sun without heat or passion.
And when the pyracantha was bare-arse naked
The birds fed winter with their purple songs.

Winter waited for *sad* sufferers to stand in a straight, rigid line:
Seasonal abnormality disorder screaming a snowstorm;
God was in His laundry, all was white with the world.
The elderly concealed congealed autumntime faces resembling
Battered cod before being deep-fried.
Little children squealed in delight, springing into action
Like cats on summer hot, corrugated tin roofs.

Spring emerged from the bowels of winter's discontent,
Shotblasting redundant words from a poet's notebook;
Changed dull days into pale apparel in just one moment.
Soft, light cumulus dream replaced hard, dark nightmare;
Summer and autumn were just a sun and a quiver away.
My upside-down umbrella
Collected only enigma and innuendo.

Robert Ensor

12

Lughnasa Light

Dusk stretches across the clock
where a rusty flowerhead on a dark stalk
edges the bank of the meadow. Late
lushness gushes out from thistle and dock.
A single celandine, July-bright, offers
a candle for the dying. Bracken concedes
to October, its amber fronds almost brittle.
The small flowers keep the flames lit,
out-of-season pale blossoms on the bramble
weighed down by late berries left to spoil.
Purplish knapweed, not yet faded, finishes
its year, its life, solitary, too.
Beyond the small trees curtained by ivy
fuchsia's now an empty nest.

Jamie O'Hallaran

Shelley in Summer

A summer June day and you turn up in my garden,
cornflowers and honeysuckle around your straw hat.
On my way to the Downs, you say, *can't stop for long.*
As if you ever could.

Mi*nd the roads*, I say, *and all the cars* ...
But you're gone, bright shadow, quick wave and goodbye.
At least there are skylarks still on the hills, though less
than there were, poor birds, hungry for stubble
lost to their winter fields.

Yet there is rapture as they fly high
and joy to be had in their song.

And of course it's the larks and your passion for flying
that brings you here again.
Clouds were your obsession and sycamore seeds –
the wind, the light, the air, the smell of a flower
you wrote in a letter –

Was that enough for you then?
Will it be enough for you now?

Budburst is earlier, duration's altered,
February offered us a false spring, and a Beast from the East
arrived in the bitter chill of March.
Pollinating insects, migratory birds, flowers that open
to frost – there is change, and confusion.

Later, gossip tells me you have left the Downs
and are well on your way to Italy and a heat wave.
No problem for me, you say, remembering Livorno's
fierce sunshine, your tower with glass on all sides.

But this is what worries me –
I know you long to see Mont Blanc, feel again
the wonder, the terror, the beauty and power.
But listen, the temperatures are rising,
glaciers melt and are breaking away.
Your magnificent white giant
is fragile.
But you never listen to advice so I won't spoil
your return with gloom. Here is a world of upheaval
for you to thrive on, score upon score of Peterloos,
and now there's a new kind of sublime –
the sublimity of technology.
Think how rapidly you could send out your words,
be ahead of the news. Outer space is yours to explore,
no more need for fire balloons or messages
in dark green bottles.

I'm glad you came to visit my garden
on this warm and scented afternoon.
You remind me there is rhythm in the seasons,
in birth, in flowering and decline,
and, as you already know Shelley, in death.

Mandy Pannett

Legacy

Then upon a time…

Nature's primordial seed fertile in flower and feather,
Life thrusted through frozen soil
And a warmth sighed over the heather.
Though an occasional loss.
Murmurs of breezy skies and birds on the wing -
An ember of hope ignited in the darkness,
When Blessed Nature began to sing.

Fire fierced overhead, thrilling clouds to vapour,
Scorching brown earth to dust - passion of the Maker.
Purpled reds revelled with tawny golds
And coupled in parched beds below;
A single day shivered in unfriendly wind.
Yet Nature's Queen, pregnant with fruitful trust,
Thrilled her potent love upon the land in tender lust.

Nature's orgy spent, its leaves turned red in tense delight
Then joined their flaxen lovers, swirling in the stormy night.
A clutch of cursed eggs in a tree - still
Trees and shrubs disrobed, as fruit plumped full of juice and
                                                          wasp eggs -
The sweet smell of earth's rotting ripened dregs.

Icy naked limbs reached in supplication to the blackened sky,
Whilst Nature's corpses reposed in her eternally breathing tomb.
One green shoot peeped then passed into darkened womb.
Brittle bones of once verdant life scattered in Pagan silence,
Whilst hungry scavengers picked amongst the protein cemetery.

Now upon a time…

Humanity, fat with decrees and laws, rules.
Sartorially suited humans demand order, votes -
With greedy fists grasping red and purple notes,
And bloated banks busting their bilious fumes, they
Bitch in surgically square rooms.

Minds of madness blast through forest, fen and field –
Our green Earth's devastation surely sealed.
Concrete flowers bloom and the toxic tarmac chokes.
Earth shudders her final painful breaths as factory filth
Vomits its sickened slurry and slaughters
Air, earth and waters.

The self-made reaper hacks, hews and cleaves
And Nature's Queen – devastated - simply grieves.

The story has been fractured,
The Maker's Dream rent in two -
Hateful pride of our human legacy.

We all need change.
Will you?

Julie Poole

Another Poem About Spring

Poets should be allowed,
like children in their earliest exercise,
to call a poem 'Spring' (no matter
that Hopkins did it better) –
Spring bounces back
where lesser themes surrender their dry stalks
to the gobbling frost,
and suddenly

the lawn lights up
like a gas ring with the purple flames of crocus;
the year's first butterfly – a brimstone – so
scatterbrained in flight
it might be the wind's toy (only today
there is no wind) passes and each particular bird
seasons with its song
the bubbling cauldron of the treetops.

Anthony Watts

Yellow Scabious

In spring, when the first shoots appeared, I wept,
and touched their little heads, and wished them well.
I wish all things well, compulsively. Reaching out
to those that cannot reach back, because human hands
can be too complicated, but seeds I understand.
I invade my garden with unnatural grief, upending
my dark like a watering can, stroking tree bark,
scraping knee to stone, hand to nettle, sticky with sap,
petting the snails, turning the soil, telling the green –
I'm done with my dying, only to turn and find my
bucket somehow full of water again, demanding
to be emptied. How long I have nourished this grief –
it seems obscene. The little seeds now taller than I am,
their sunny faces untroubled by the human beneath.
I cannot change in a season, but I do understand the pull
of light. Why else would I reach up, caress their petals,
promise again to put down the scythe? However hard
I try, my hands go numb. I am distracted by the pain
of holding on. But look, how little effort is needed
to save my life. In a flurry of wind, I am showered
in gossamer petals, and I laugh in unexpected delight.
I know then that I will find them again next spring,
tiny in the earth, unknowingly beloved. However
light or heavy my heart, I will wish them well,
I promise.

Amy Wolstenholme

Judge's Comments on winning poems

Mood Disorder
This was brave and honest writing; a beautiful yet sad poem
with undertones of determination and faith. It read so easily and
the analogies and metaphors are fantastic, 'like leaves
imprisoned in winter's strass, I cannot escape the white coats of
snow.' Strength and fragility are communicated at the same
time. I love the author's interpretation of the brief and, more
than anything, this poem stays with me. It makes me *feel.*

Winter Has A Wish For You
A beautifully written and crafted poem. Images are full of
originality and creativity. Nothing is predictable or clichéd.
Packed with description in spite of its brevity, no words are
wasted here. It explored the brief in the most wonderful way.

getting the summer clothes out of storage
The open honesty of this poem really moved me. I love the way
the author uses clothes to tell the story. It has both light and
shade despite its sadness. Beautifully written with a wonderful
simplicity to it. It stayed with me for many days after reading.

Here She Comes
This accessible poem was filled with wonderful analogies,
metaphors and exquisite description, creating colourful images.
Alliteration provided a lovely rhythm.

Liz Barnes